Online Marketing Fundamentals

PAUL RAINMAKER

ISBN-10: 1542371376
ISBN-13: 978-1542371377

FOR LEAH

A few years ago, we were shopping at a thrift sale for a local church. You saw a little toy car that was an exact replica, down to the color and model, of the automobile that I often, loudly, dreamed about. You, at 9 years old, bought the toy car and gave it to me because you wanted me to have my dream! That meant so much to me. For the gazillion ways that you've shown me that you believe in me, domo arigatou gozaimashita.

TABLE OF CONTENTS

ACKNOWLEDGEMENTS

There have been many online marketers, authors and mentors that have influenced my career and ultimately, shaped my success. I owe them all a ton of gratitude. Thank you Todd Brown, Jay Abraham, Roy H. Williams, Rich Schefren, Frank Kern, Perry Marshall, Bryan Todd, Jeff Walker, Cuzin Andy Jenkins, Don Crowther, Ryan Levesque, Russell Brunson, Brendon Burchard, GKIC, Ryan Deiss, Perry Belcher, Eben (DD) Pagan, Yanik Silver, Jeff Johnson, Derek Gehl, Corey Rudl, Tony Robbins, Jonah Berger, Mom, Dad and my entire family for blazing the trail and illuminating my path.

HOW TO USE THIS BOOK

It isn't necessary for you to read this book sequentially from beginning to end. Every chapter of this book introduces a different concept of online marketing and is self-contained. So if you prefer, you can read the chapters in any order that you'd like!

You can find supplemental information by visiting PaulRainmaker.com/resources

1 INTRODUCTION

Before and during much of the 1990s, anyone with a little HTML knowledge could create a website. These days, creating a professional website requires the collaboration of professionals with a wide variety of college degrees and expertise. You might need graphic designers, front end coders, back end developers, networking professionals, search engine optimizers, copywriters, email marketers, conversion rate optimizers, paid traffic managers, social media professionals, animators, analysts and project managers to help you create a modern website experience. My how times have changed!

Over the past 20 years, I have held every technical and creative position within website development and digital marketing companies. I've witnessed the evolution of these industries first-hand. I've seen trends, tactics and technologies come and go.

And then, one day, it all just came together. I began applying everything that I had come to learn and started generating mountains of profits for my clients. That was several years ago. Since then, I've helped businesses, entrepreneurs and the clients of marketing agencies generate multiple millions of dollars in revenue.

I want to share my experience with you. I'm hoping to impart sound, fundamental, Internet marketing strategies that will help you establish and grow your online enterprises. As I've often said to clients, this knowledge does not benefit anyone if it stays inside of my head. I hope you find it useful.

Wishing you the best of luck,
Paul Rainmaker

2 LANDING PAGE OPTIMIZATION

Have you heard of the term "A/B Split-Testing"? It refers to a method of progressively improving the performance of a step in your marketing sequence. You can split-test almost any element of your marketing, from advertisements to opt-in forms to emails. You start with an "A" version, create an alternate "B" version and measure the performance between the two. This process is sometimes referred to as Conversion Rate Optimization (CRO).

Smart online marketers are constantly tweaking and testing their primary landing pages. Google Analytics allows you to split-test your pages, or you could use a service such as Unbounce, InstaPage, Optimizely, ClickFunnels or

Visual Website Optimizer.

Landing pages are critical to the success of your online marketing efforts. You can send all of the traffic in the world to your landing page but if it isn't converting, then your business won't be generating the vital leads and sales necessary to stay profitable.

Some landing pages convert at the rate of 18% and that is considered good. Other pages convert at 38% and that is considered normal. It all depends on the competitiveness of your niche, the quality of your traffic, the stage of awareness that your prospect is currently in, the effectiveness of your copywriting and how you actually define a conversion.

Start by split-testing two vastly different versions of your page before you move on to testing the smaller, subtler elements of your landing page. Each version of the page should have at least 250 impressions to properly establish the performance rate.

Copy

When you are split-testing your copy, you should initially focus on your headlines and subheadlines before refining your copy in support of them. Your headlines should reach out in empathy to your prospects and convey that you understand the problem situation that they are experiencing. Subheadlines should be used to introduce the unique method that your product or service employs in order to solve the problem that your prospects are experiencing.

Congruency between ads and their corresponding landing pages is important. Make sure that your landing pages fulfill the promise made in your ads. For example, if your ad hinted at a specific benefit of your product or service, then your landing page should reiterate that benefit and expand on the claim.

Another important element of your landing pages are your Calls To Action (CTAs). As often as possible, you should use personal, affirmative language in your CTAs. So instead of writing “Get it Now” as your CTA, try “Get Mine Now” instead.

Design and Layout

Beautiful design doesn’t correspond with higher conversion rates. I wish it did. I’m sorry to say it, but time after time, I’ve seen great design get outperformed by less attractive versions of the same landing page. There are just certain elements that seem to generate the most conversions. For example, non-scripty fonts, also known as sans serif fonts, such as Arial or Helvetica, do perform quite well. They're just easier on the eyes to read quickly.

There must be congruency between the design of your ad and the design of your landing page. The color scheme should be the same. The font should be the same. The images should be the same or closely related. It's a subtle way of letting your prospect know that they have landed on the right webpage.

Speaking of subtlety and congruency, you can use visual cues to suggest and reinforce your Calls To Action. You could use arrows to point to your information capturing form. I've also seen pictures of people pointing and/or looking directly at the form. (See the image on the next page.) Most commonly, I've seen the use of bright, eye-attracting colors for the submit button.

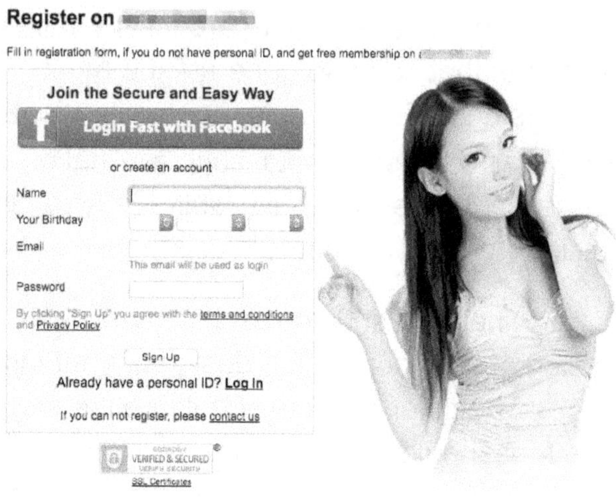

Have you ever heard of the term 'first fold'? It's an old expression used by newspaper publishers. The first fold refers to elements that are visible on the front page above the line where the newspaper would fold. In web design, it refers to all elements that are visible *without scrolling* when the webpage first loads. Since you may have just a few seconds for your landing page to make an impact, it is advantageous to include the most important elements of the page within the first fold. I strongly recommend placing an information-capturing form and your first Call To Action in plain sight in the first fold of your landing pages.

Images

The images on your landing pages should obviously be related to your offer. If you are presenting a picture of your product, then make sure that your product is the central focus of the image and is not being diminished by something that is happening in the background. Images that are blurry or pixilated convey a lack of quality, so please make sure that your images are clear at all resolutions.

While product images are good, images of people that are using the product or are enjoying the benefits of using the product/service are better. In addition, photographs of people work best when everybody is looking directly into the camera.

Trust And Credibility

When creating a sales page, it is advantageous to include images of trust icons and guarantee seals. A "secure" trust icon, for example, serves to assure your prospects that you are using secure transmission protocols and that their information is safe. Guarantee seals are useful as visual representations of your return policy. If you are accredited by a third party association such as the Better Business Bureau, you should include an image of their logo. Trust imagery serves to reinforce your trustworthiness and definitely boosts conversion rates!

While we are on the subject of trust, your terms of service (TOS) page and privacy policy page should be easily accessible and clearly written. Nothing scares off a prospect faster than convoluted policies and excessive legalese.

Finally, if you are going to use testimonials, please make sure that you include the name, position and a picture of the source. Anonymous quotes just aren't believable and will probably cause you to lose the conversion.

Chapter Summary

1. Copy

    - Focus on headlines and subheadlines.
    - Fulfill the promise of your ads.
    - Use Calls To Action.

2. Design and Layout

    - Use non-scripty fonts.
    - Ensure congruency between the design of the ad and the design of the landing page.
    - Place forms and CTAs in the first-fold.

3. Images

    - Use images of people whenever possible.
    - Include trust imagery.

4. Simplify Privacy Policy and Terms of Service.

5. Use testimonials that are credible.

3 SEARCH ENGINE OPTIMIZATION

When you ask a search engine for information, you are submitting a keyword and receiving Search Engine Results Pages (SERPs) in response. Search Engine Optimization (SEO) can be defined as the art and science of getting a webpage to prominently appear in SERPs. The ultimate accomplishment in SEO, therefore, is achieving a first-position ranking on the first page of SERPs for keywords that best describe your business, products or services.

There is much disinformation out there about what SEO techniques actually work and which ones are either outdated or outright lies. More than anything, Google and other search engines just want to see authentic, original content. If you have a deep knowledge of a specific topic, then you can get your content ranked for the keywords of your niche. It really is that simple.

I wanted to introduce the topic of SEO early in this book because it will take the longest amount of time to implement. It takes a considerable effort to create quality content and you need to have a plan for how to implement and organize that content on your website.

Since Google is the largest search engine on the planet, I am going to teach you how to make your website Google friendly. If these techniques work for Google, then you can be certain that they will work for achieving rank on other search engines as well.

PageSpeed

Pagespeed is important. Google recognizes that if your webpage takes forever to load, then your visitor is very likely to leave your website. But guess what? The single greatest determinant for how quickly your webpage loads has nothing to do with your website at all! It is the quality of your website hosting service that matters most. So before you invest your precious resources into everything else that we are about to discuss, make sure that you are hosting your website with a quality hosting provider. If you need help in selecting one, visit my resources page at PaulRainmaker.com/resources for more information.

To test the speed of your webpage, use Google's free pagespeed tester located at developers.google.com/speed/pagespeed/insights/ What's great about this tool is that you will receive actionable insights on how to improve your webpage performance. Just remember that this tool does not measure the overall speed of your entire website. You will have to test your pages one at a time. If you would like a more detailed analysis for how your page performs, you can visit webpagetest.org

Mobile Friendly

Not only should your webpages load quickly, they should also render well on mobile devices. When your website detects and adapts to browsers on mobile devices, it is considered responsive. Make sure that when you select your website template (or your Wordpress theme) that it is considered to be responsive. Google does penalize nonresponsive websites.

You may have heard about AMP technology. Accelerated Mobile Pages is an open source, HTML framework developed by Google. Webpages created with AMP load much faster than traditional webpages. In addition, Google is currently showing pages built with AMP *first* in their search engine results pages. I strongly recommend integrating AMP into your website development cycle. If you are a WordPress user, it's as simple as adding and configuring the AMP plug-in.

Free Google Tools

You should definitely install the Google Webmaster Tools code onto every page of your website. The Webmaster Tools interface will be very helpful in suggesting the proper courses of action necessary to make your website more SEO friendly.

Would you like to see how Google views and displays the individual pages of your website? If so, you can perform a site: (pronounced, "site colon") search. Open up your web browser, find the Google search bar and enter "site: YourDomain.com". Google will return a list of every page on your domain that it has crawled and indexed. This is useful in determining how your page titles and descriptions are displayed. If you discover that Google has indexed a page that you don't want to be publicly available, you can specifically disallow that page.

Robots.txt

Speaking of disallowing pages, have you ever heard of a robot.txt file? It is a text file that instructs bots, spiders and various web crawlers as to your preferences for indexing certain pages and sections of your website. Of course, not all spiders follow and respect these instructions, but Google and other reputable search engines will.

To see if you have a robot.txt file and to check its contents, go to "YourDomain.com/ robot.txt". If the file doesn't exist, then you are essentially giving permission for the bots to crawl and index every file on your entire domain. But let's say that you don't want any of the files in your images folder to be indexed. You would create an entry in your robots.txt file that looks like this: "disallow /images/". Note that you are allowed one entry per line.

I should mention that the first line of your

robots.txt file will be "user-agent: *". This means that all of your disallow instructions apply to all bots and crawlers that visit your website. Instead of an asterisk, it is possible to address each bot individually and by name, but the asterisk keeps things simple.

Yoast For WordPress

If you are using WordPress to create your website, then I highly recommend the Yoast plug-in. After choosing a specific keyword that you want to optimize a page for, Yoast helps you place that keyword into the various parts of your page enough times to achieve pagerank. It's very helpful. The Yoast plug-in will give you specific instructions as to the actual location on the page that you need to place your keyword.

Backlinks

Success with backlinks really boils down to the number of recent, quality links that are pointing to your webpage. What has changed, over the years, is the definition of what constitutes a quality link.

Previously, there were no requirements on the quality of the link. All that mattered was the number of links to your website. Then, as a metric of gravity or weight was introduced, a link from one prominent website could be worth ten links from a lesser website. To a certain extent, that system of backlink gravity is still in play. So if you can get your website featured in a prominent blog such as the Huffington Post, you will have earned some valuable consideration from Google's search ranking algorithm.

Today, search engines also assign great importance to the number of links to your content that are shared via social media and email. So make sure that you include multiple links to share your content within all of your webpages and emails.

As you can see, it is very important to have links that point to your website. In fact, it is so important that some SEO agencies only focus on acquiring these links. But not all links are equal. Some are undesirable and others are detrimental. So how do you find out who is linking to your website? Just enter your website URL into one of the dozens of 'free backlink checkers' available online. If you want something more sophisticated, use a service such as Ahrefs.com or Majestic.com.

If some questionable domain links to your website and you wish to disassociate your business from it, just go to your Google Webmaster Tools interface, enter the domain and disavow it.

SSL

Another simple but effective way to stay on Google's good side is to implement SSL on your entire website. The Secure Sockets Layer adds encryption and security. It is the protocol that is used to securely transmit your private information across the Internet when you are making a purchase. These days, Google recommends that ALL pages on your website employ SSL technology. It's easy for your website developer to implement. When all of your webpages begin with HTTPS instead of HTTP, then you have successfully implemented SSL.

Review

Whew! You have just covered the fundamentals of Search Engine Optimization. Here's a quick recap:

- Maximize PageSpeed
- Make sure that your website is Mobile Friendly
- Install Google Webmaster Tools
- Use the site: search
- Configure your robots.txt file
- Use the Yoast Plug-in for WordPress
- Gain quality Backlinks
- Add encryption and security with SSL

In the next section, you will learn how to structure your content in a way that positions your website as an authority. You will learn what is at the heart of modern day search engine optimization. This is what really works for SEO today.

Authenticity

It is all about authenticity. If you are an expert in your profession and you genuinely have knowledge to share, you will have no problem in getting your pages ranked. Google just wants to see people consume your content. So they assign great importance to the number of pages someone views on your website and the length of time your visitors stay on each page. And if your visitors share a page from your website, that is also very good.

Keywords, of course, are at the very heart of the search engine optimization process. Everyone is trying to get their pages ranked for specific keywords so that they may capture a fraction of the naturally occurring traffic that these keywords generate. But it is not as much of a head-to-head competition as it may seem. There are plenty of variations of the same keyword for many websites to be wildly successful. Also, your geographic location does influence the search results that you receive. For example, if you search for a tax lawyer, you are going to receive a list of local tax lawyers versus a list of tax lawyers that are located on the other side of the country.

Let's say you are a food critic and want to start a new section of your website or blog that is dedicated to hamburgers. You have decided to optimize your blog for the keywords "best burger" and "best hamburger". Now, when you create your content, you should include one of these keywords into your page title, page description, keyword tag, alt tags, anchor tags, headlines, link text and copy. If your blog is a Wordpress blog, then you should create a category called "best hamburgers" and a tag called "burgers". Professional SEOs also include keywords in the name of the images on the page. You don't necessarily have to keep the words "best" and "burger" together but they should be in close proximity to each other. For example, if you write about the best guacamole burger, that is fine.

Keyword-Themed Content Silos

How you organize all of this content is *most important.* It is critical that you arrange your content into a hierarchy of semantically related posts. Some folks refer to this as building keyword-themed content silos. It means that all of your supporting posts will be nested under a single master post. For every keyword that you are seeking to achieve page rank for, you should have at least 7 supporting posts.

In our food critic example, the master post would be located at YourDomain.com/best-hamburgers. Your supporting post on jalapeno cheddar burgers would be located at YourDomain.com/best-hamburgers/best-jalapeno-cheddar-burger-ever and your post on the best burger in Texas would be located at YourDomain.com/best-hamburgers/best-burger-in-Texas. Do you see how this works?

If you, as a food critic, get tired of burgers and want to optimize your blog around keywords related to ice cream, then you would create another hierarchy of keyword related content. Your master post might be titled 'ice-cream' and your could have supporting posts that are titled 'my-favorite-pistachio-ice-cream' and 'i-scream-for-ice-cream'.

Keywords	Domain	Master Post	Supporting Post
Best hamburgers, best burgers	YourDomain.com	/best-hamburgers/	Best-jalapeno-cheddar-burger-ever
Best hamburgers, best burgers	YourDomain.com	/best-hamburgers/	Best-burger-in-Texas
Ice cream	YourDomain.com	/ice-cream/	My-favorite-pistachio-ice-cream
Ice cream	YourDomain.com	/ice-cream/	I-scream-for-ice-cream

Interlinking

All of your related posts should be interlinked. Every supporting post, perhaps towards the bottom of the copy, should link to the master post. Bonus points if the text of the link contains your keywords. If your master post contains links to your supporting posts, that is great. If some of your supporting posts link to each other, that is also very good. Not all posts have to link to every other post, but it should be clear that your content is related.

The future of SEO

SEO is a constantly evolving cat and mouse game between webmasters and search engines. But there are trends in how people are changing in their use of technology that may one day permanently alter this.

More and more people are consuming content from within apps and app content curation is not based on traditional search engine optimization rankings. Moreover, how these apps are actually discovered also has little to do with modern SEO. As a matter fact, there are actually separate techniques related to App Store Optimization (ASO).

Major social networks such as Facebook and Twitter have their own internal search engines. More often than not, when you read news and articles on these social networks, you will not leave the platform at all. Once again, how this content is ranked and made discoverable from within the specific social network has nothing to do with traditional SEO ranking methods.

There is also the increasing trend of verbally asking your devices for search results. It's one thing to optimize your website for keywords such as 'best lasagna in Manhattan' but how can you optimize it for the situation when someone asks their phone to 'find Italian close by'? Voice activated searches are definitely complicating the search engine optimization landscape.

Based upon these and other trends in how people are using technology, I can say with absolute certainty that SEO will look substantially different in 10 years than it does today.

4 HOW TO WRITE EFFECTIVE COPY

There are tons of books that have been written on the subject of copywriting. Some of the all-time great copywriters in history include David Ogilvy, Clayton Makepeace, Gary Halbert, John Carlton, Gary Bencivenga, John Caples, Claude Hopkins, Eugene Schwartz and Bill Jayme. I definitely recommend reading everything that you can from them.

In my opinion, the most important facet of copywriting is to realize that you should NOT write about your business, products or services. Absolutely not. You should always write about your prospects and customers. What problems are your prospects experiencing? If you can get them to imagine a perfect life as a result of using your products or services, then you will have gained a very loyal customer indeed.

The Central Promise

Let's start with the very reason why you are in business. What is THE concept behind your product or service? I'm not talking about your unique selling proposition. I am asking you to articulate how your product or service transforms or improves the lives of your customers. All of your copywriting should revolve around this one central concept.

For example, there is a famous pizza chain that promises "fresh, hot pizza in 30 minutes or less." This is the core concept of their marketing and, indeed, of their entire business. Everything that this pizza chain does revolves around this one central concept.

If you have multiple products or services, then you should develop a central promise for each one. Start with the results that your prospect desires more than anything.

I have a client with a proprietary, online, piano instruction method. His prospects just want to play their favorite songs on the piano, without taking a bunch of lessons about complicated music theory. His promise addresses that frustration and his prospects desired outcome: "Would you like to play your favorite songs on the piano without learning mountains of music theory? You can transform from a lesson taker into a song player with the new Magic Music Maker Method for piano!"

It is very important for you to express exactly what you are offering your prospects. What is the main idea behind your product or service? In addition to the practical benefits, does it solve an emotional need of your prospects? Can you sum it up in one or two sentences? Once you have found your central concept, you will be able to write effective, compelling copy.

Persuasion

Influence and persuasion are ultimately about getting your prospect to change their mind. You want them to transform from the belief that they are a prospect into the belief that they are a customer. So you must supply them, educate them and indoctrinate them with all of the information they need to make that change.

Let's say I have a toothache. I need to

know that you are a trained, licensed dentist with an appointment ready for me. And I need to know that if I did nothing, my pain will only increase. That's it! I'm sold.

What does your prospect need to know about you, your services or about their own situation to make your offer seem irresistible? How can you use credibility, logic and emotion to make your offer truly persuasive?

Features vs. Benefits

Speaking of logic versus emotion, I want to explain the difference between features and benefits. Features are based on facts. If I'm selling a computer, and it features 2 GB of RAM, that is a fact. The benefit of this feature is how that 2 GB of RAM will improve the speed of your computing experience. Your software will load faster. Your graphics will render quicker. Those are all benefits.

Good marketers include both features and benefits into their copywriting. Just remember to always frame your features in terms of the benefits it will impart to your prospects.

I'm not sure who coined this phrase, but it neatly sums up the difference between them: "Features tell, Benefits sell."

Message Structure

While all of these copywriting concepts are important, this next one is huge. If you get this one right, then your business will explode with profits and may even out-live you. All brilliant copywriters answer these 3 questions in order: Why? How? & What?

It doesn't matter if you are writing a 275 page manifesto, a long-form sales letter or a short, little Adwords haiku. All of the most effective presentations in the world follow this simple formula.

Have you ever seen those three or four part video campaigns that introduce a new product? The next time you see one, notice how the first video is all about the 'why'. (As in, why some problem exists and why some entrepreneur is out to solve that problem.) Then, notice how the second video is all about the 'how'. (How is the problem going to be solved?) Finally, in the third video, notice how it answers the 'what' question. (As in, what is the product that will remedy the situation?)

I want you to go online, right now, and find a video presentation called "Start with Why" by Simon Sinek. Let him drop some knowledge on you. Then, put this information into practice today.

Now that you are aware of how successful businesses structure their marketing messages, you may begin to see it everywhere. It is actually quite common when you know what you are looking for. If it has worked for all of them, surely it will work for you as well. Put this information into practice today!

Calls To Action

Did you notice my previous statement? How it commands you to perform a task immediately? Did you notice how it has appeared more than once? These are the qualities of Calls To Action.

Calls To Action suggest and compel your prospects to take some desired action, like clicking the order button or entering an email address. Do not be afraid to include them in your copywriting. They might just provide the nudge your prospects need to take the next step.

Writing Copy For Adwords

Adwords text ads are some of the most difficult ads to write because you are limited to a small amount of characters with which to convey your entire marketing message. The first line of your ad, the headline, is limited to just 35 characters and the second & third lines are limited to 25 characters. That's not much to work with!

Your headline should always reach out to your prospects and reflect their intentions. For example, if you were writing an ad for someone that is searching for 'lobster bisque recipes', then your headline should say something like: "Get Lobster Bisque Recipes HERE." That's pretty straightforward, right?

The second line of your ad should convey something emotional, such as "Savory, like grandma used to make." This is the perfect time to insert a benefit of what you are advertising. In contrast to the second line, the third line should contain a feature or something factual such as "Find 36 unique bisque recipes."

It is always best to include the actual search term, also known as the keyword, into the copy of your text ad. It is more than just reflecting the searchers intentions. Google will actually highlight those search terms in the copy of your ad. So the more times you can use the keyword in your ad copy, the better. It will greatly increase the chances that your ad will be clicked.

> Adwords recently rolled out "Expanded Text Ads". This is good news! These ads have slightly higher character limits. The expanded headline has a limit of 30 characters. The second line also has a limit of 30 characters, but the third line has a limit of 80 characters!

Landing Page Congruency

If you consider the headline of your ads to be promises, then you must make sure that your landing pages adequately fulfill that promise. If I click on an ad about a specific product, than I expect to be taken to the product information page and not to the business homepage. Some of the best performing landing pages actually restate the headline of the ad in the landing page copy. It's a great way to continue the conversation, so to speak.

This concept is not just limited to the copywriting either. If you are running visual banner ads, then your landing page should be constructed using the same font and color scheme as your ads. Maintaining congruency is critical to building trust. Make sure you are paying attention to all the little details, ok?

Writing Copy For Video

When you create a video ad, it is especially important to immediately grab the attention of your prospects. You only have a few seconds to create that first impression. The best thing you can do is reach out to your ideal prospect by stating your core concept in the form of a question. For example, let's say you are creating a video to promote your 10 part, wine-making tutorials. You would start your video by asking the question, "Would you like to learn how to make wine from your home in 10 easy step-by-step lessons?"

It is also advisable to announce the contents of each video. I'm sure you've heard people say, "In this video, I'm going to show you X, Y and Z." When you let your prospects know exactly what they can expect from your video, you'll have a much greater chance of having your ideal prospect stay and watch the video in its entirety.

When creating videos for Facebook, you will have one additional obstacle to overcome. You see, Facebook automatically mutes your videos while they are being displayed. Meaning, your prospects actually have to click on your video to hear what you are saying. So what can you do?

I've seen some marketers wave their arms around in the beginning of their videos, hoping to catch your curiosity and attention. I've seen others cup their ears, implying a 'Can you hear this?' pantomime. The important element here is to use motion to attract the attention of your prospect. I've also seen actual text at the beginning of some videos which simply state, 'Click to hear this message.'

Use whatever works for you. Use your creativity and have fun!

Affirmative Copy On The Order Form

This is an old school, direct response marketing technique that has been around since the early days of mail order. But it is just as effective in the online world as it is in the print world. Have you ever seen an order form with a little check box next to a paragraph that reads something like this:

"Yes! I want the secrets to building wealth. Show me how to explode my profits with your secret formula. Send me the 12 CDs, the 184 page transcript, the DVD of the live presentation PLUS my 2 valuable bonus CDs. Additionally, send me the monthly newsletter so that I'll stay up to date on the latest strategies. I understand that I will be conveniently billed in monthly installments and can cancel at anytime."

Using affirmative copy in your order forms is sure to influence your prospects into buying. Try it and see!

Chapter Summary

1. Formulate the Central Promise. How does your product or service fulfill the needs and wants of your prospects?
2. Use Persuasion to turn your prospect into a customer.
3. Present facts in terms of Features and Benefits.
4. Design your copy using the Why, How & What message structure.
5. Create Calls To Action to compel your prospects into taking your desired next step.
6. Use Adwords to convey your marketing message:
   a. Headlines reflect your prospects intentions.
   b. Line 2 illustrates a benefit of your product or service.
   c. Line 3 mentions a fact about your product or service.
   d. Include keywords in your copy.
7. Landing Pages must be congruent with your ad. Use the same headline, image, colors, font, etc.
8. Grab attention quickly in your videos by restating your Central Promise in the form of a question.
9. Use Affirmative Copy on your order forms.

5 HOW TO TRACK PERFORMANCE

In the late 1800s, John Wanamaker, a US department store merchant, was quoted as saying, “Half the money I spend on advertising is wasted; the trouble is I don’t know which half.” These days, nothing could be further from the truth.

Modern reporting technologies, properly implemented, can track every little detail of a prospects’ interaction with your advertising campaigns and website. This is accomplished by the use of scripts and pixels that are strategically calibrated and placed into your marketing funnels.

I am always surprised at the sheer number of businesses that either track their results poorly or not at all. Measuring the performance of your individual marketing campaigns and specific website pages is absolutely essential! There is no excuse for not doing this.

Google Analytics

The most common reporting tool is Google analytics, which is free. It is also one of the most robust reporting tools. Analytics tracks all sources of traffic to your website - no matter if it comes from an email newsletter, social media, a specific web address, or your online advertising campaigns. It tracks what part of the world your visitors come from, how they navigate your website and how long they stay on each page. There is even a real-time feature that will show you how many people are visiting your website right now.

Google Analytics provides you with a heatmap of any page on your site. This heatmap will show you what elements of the page are clicked on most frequently. So if, for example, an image is getting clicked on, then you know that you should create some type of response to those clicks. Heatmaps are also useful in revealing where on your page your visitors are reading to and where they are dropping off from, so you know the exact point on the page that requires improvement.

Most importantly, you can configure Goals in Analytics to accurately measure performance. For example, when a user subscribes or makes a purchase and is taken to a "thank you" page, you can track that as a conversion. Furthermore, these Goals can be imported into Adwords so that you can track which ad and specific keyword brought you that conversion.

When you can track all sources of your conversions this way, it makes business decisions easy. John Wanamaker would be envious of the reporting tools available today. To get started, go to Analytics.Google.com and sign in with your Google business account.

> Pro tip: It is strongly advised that you unite all of your Google services under a single Google account. That means your YouTube, G+, Adwords, Analytics, Tag Manager, Gmail, Webmaster Tools, Google Docs and Google Business Page, etc, should all be accessible via a single login. Not only will that eliminate confusion, but it will unlock special and helpful menus within your various Google properties.

> If you already have multiple Google accounts, you can call Google Customer Service to consolidate them. However, if you're just getting started, you can begin with Google.com/Business

The Google Analytics Script

The "Admin" tab is the place to begin configuring your Analytics account. Click on "Tracking Info" and select "Tracking Code" to view your Analytics script. In order to get all of the benefits that Analytics has to offer, you will have to place this script into the <head> tag of every page of your website. Please Note: the default Analytics script is configured for use on one domain only. If you plan on tracking multiple domains or additional subdomains, the script will have to be modified slightly.

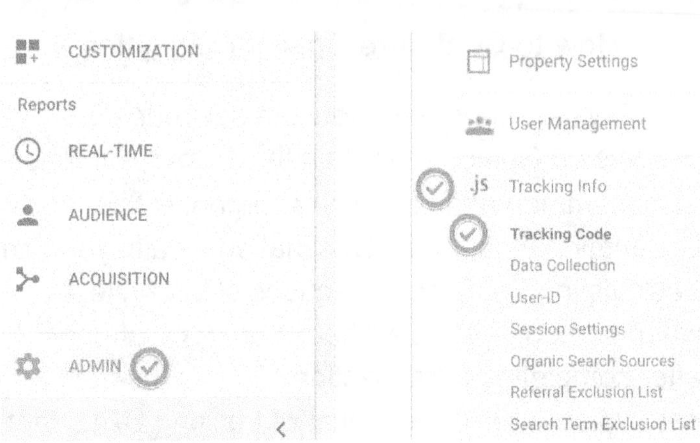

Connecting Analytics and AdWords

You can also connect your Adwords account with your Analytics account here in the Admin tab. Select the "Adwords Linking" option and be prepared to enter your 10 digit Adwords account number. Once that is done, login to your Adwords account and select "Conversions" from the Tools menu. Then, click on the "Analytics" option from the left-side menu. Select the goals that you wish to bring into Adwords and click Import.

How to Configure Goals in Analytics

Most importantly, you can set your conversion Goals from within the Admin tab. The most common and useful type of goal is the Destination Goal. With Destination Goals, you can track visitors to different sections of your site, or when someone visits a "thank you" type of page after completing a transaction. Here's the tricky part: you will have the option of tracking URLs that either "Equal" or "Contain" or "Begin with" specific terms.

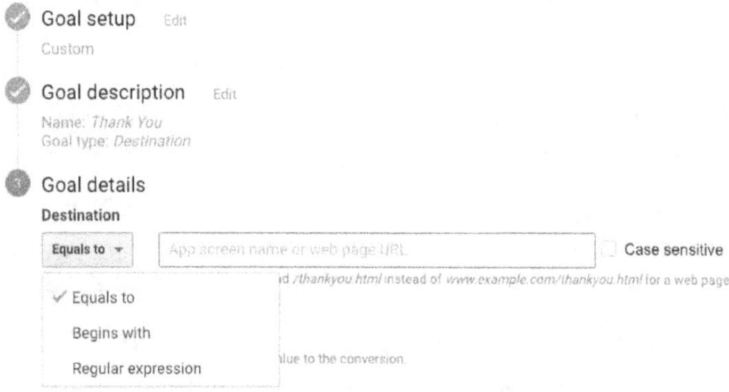

Equal is used for specifying exact page URLs. This option is case sensitive, meaning that you will have to type in capital and lowercase letters exactly as they appear on your website. Remember to include the .html portion of the URL.

If your website or shopping cart software dynamically appends additional information onto the URL, then you must use either the "Contains" option or the "Begins with" option. The "Contains" option allows you to specify keywords that appear in the URL. So if your transaction success page contains the words "order-confirmation", you can simply input "order-confirmation" and Analytics will track all visitors to any webpage with "order-confirmation" as part of the URL.

The "Begins with" option allows you to specify a beginning portion of the URL. For example, if you have multiple webpages within the YourDomain.com/TrackThis folder, or if your shopping cart software appends information to your YourDomain.com/Order-Confirmation page, Analytics can be configured to track all visitors to any URL that begins with your specified input.

Obviously, Google Analytics is very powerful and can be configured in many ways to sort and report the information collected. But the Analytics isn't the only reporting script that you should place on your website.

The Facebook Pixel

Just like Analytics, Facebook has a script that is to be placed within the <head> tag of all pages of your website. Unlike Analytics, it doesn't need to be modified for use on multiple domains or subdomains.

Each Facebook pixel corresponds to one Facebook Ad Account. To find your pixel, first go to the "Pixel" page within your Facebook Ad Account. Then (see below) select the "View Pixel Code" option from the Actions menu.

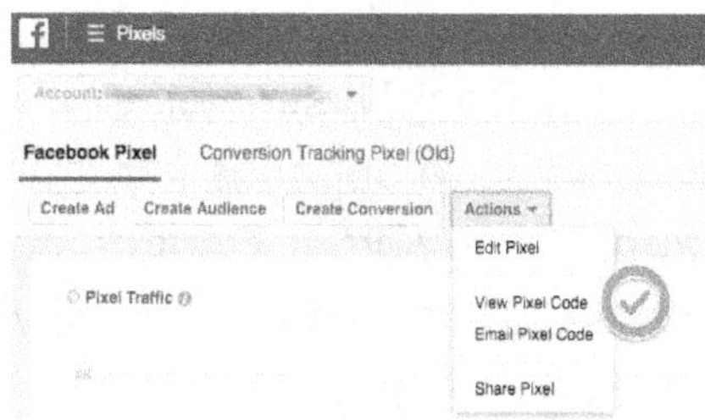

Conversion Tracking in Facebook

Tracking conversions in Facebook is actually quite easy. First, go to the "Custom Conversions" page from the Facebook Ad Manager interface Then, click on the "Create Custom Conversion" button and enter the URL that you would like to track. The same rules, as discussed before, regarding “Contains” versus “Equals” apply in Facebook as well.

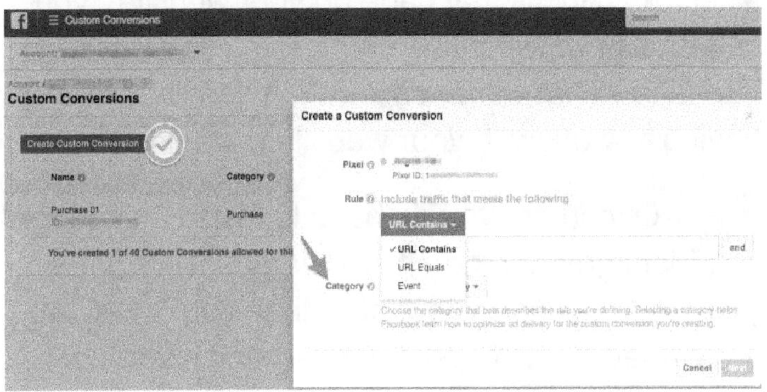

When creating your custom conversion, Facebook gives you the option of selecting the category of conversion that you are creating. This is important. You must remember the type of conversion that you select for your custom conversion, as you will need this information later when you are compiling your results.

Google Tag Manager

The Google Tag Manager greatly simplifies the process of having to add your individual pixels into the code of your website pages. This is especially useful if you have multiple third party pixels to implement. Using Google Tag Manager, you can add, modify and delete your website pixels without actually having to touch your website HTML at all. So if you want to modify a pixel for an individual page on your website, you can do it from within the Google Tag Manager interface. That's a lot easier than constantly having to work with your website code, isn't it?

Of course, you do have to install the Google Tag Manager into the <head> tag of every page of your website initially, but after that, you're set. To get started, go to google.com/analytics/tag-manager/

One of the most useful features of Google Tag Manager is the ability to delay the firing of your pixels. When I say fire, I mean that the pixel code has been executed. You see, there is a difference between somebody who immediately bounces from your landing page versus somebody that actually reads the content. If you delay the firing of your pixel by, say 15 seconds, then you know that you will be collecting statistics about a prospect that is at least familiar with your offer. It is especially useful for managing your remarketing budget.

UTM Tags

Universal Tag Manager tags are something entirely different from anything we have previously discussed. They can help you track the specific sources, campaigns and individual ads of your website traffic, but they don't use a pixel to do so.

UTM tags are appended onto the destination URL that you use in your ads. The tags are then interpreted by Analytics (as well as other reporting platforms) and will appear in your reports. So you can use UTM tags to determine which campaigns or ads are performing the best.

UTM tags are user defined and you can create as many as you like. For example, you can create a tags to track traffic sources, campaigns, audience targeting and ad creative. It's all up to you.

So where can you create your UTM tags? Good question! Adwords, Facebook and other advertising platforms give you the ability to set your UTM tags when you are uploading your ad creative. We'll get to the specifics of this when we discuss ad creation.

Of course, you have to setup your reporting

dashboard to display this information. Fortunately, Analytics readily displays the information contained within the UTM_Source and UTM_Medium tags. Therefore, the easiest way to make use of UTM tags is to confine your use of them to the Source and Medium UTM tags.

There's one potential caveat here. If you are using a URL shortener, then it is almost certain that your UTM tags will be discarded before your visitor reaches your website.

6 FACEBOOK ADVERTISING

While Google AdWords has long been considered the gold standard of pay-per-click (PPC) advertising, Facebook PPC advertising is certainly a second titan of the industry.

With over 1/7 of the entire worlds' population having an account on Facebook, there's no shortage of prospective customers and clients. However, since your advertisements will appear in the newsfeed of your prospects, which is considered to be a form of personal space, you must follow a different etiquette in order to promote successfully.

By implementing strict rules and guidelines for advertisers, Facebook has been very protective of the quality and integrity of your newsfeed. This is why you don't see promotions about dating or weight loss supplements that are obnoxious and in poor taste. It's why you don't see exaggerated claims or gimmicky imagery. I'm actually glad that they do this.

I don't participate in questionable marketing efforts because I believe in being helpful. I endorse the idea that not only should your products or services raise the quality of life for your clients, but your marketing should as well. It's an attitude that naturally integrates with Facebook's marketing policies. You see, being helpful works . . . in advertising, on Facebook and in life!

When you promote a case study, whitepaper or blog post on Facebook, that content must be helpful. Sure, it may be promoting your company but, in doing so, it should be raising the awareness of your prospects to their situation and to their possible options. The basic strategy here is to prove yourself to be helpful before you ask for the sale. It's not any different than getting to know someone before asking them to marry you. Obviously, remarketing is a major component of this approach. Since we cover remarketing in a different chapter, let's focus on the initial campaign, ok?

PowerEditor

If you aren't already using the Facebook Power Editor to implement your campaigns, then you should immediately begin doing so. Power Editor is currently available to users of the Chrome Browser only, although I would expect that to change and expand in the future.

The Facebook Power Editor offers you advanced features that are simply unavailable in the regular Facebook Ad Manager interface. It also gives you a more intuitive means of implementing your campaigns. Power Editor allows you to make multiple changes to your various campaigns all at once, which will definitely save you time. You can even see and download your performance data from within the Power Editor interface. I could go on, but I think you get the idea: Start using the Facebook Power Editor today!

Campaign Objectives

In chapter 5, you learned how to create and install the Facebook pixel onto your site. This pixel is an invaluable resource to your Facebook marketing because it actually learns. It's true! The more conversions your pixel records, the better your campaigns will perform in targeting your ideal prospects.

This does imply, however, that your Facebook pixel must be trained to seek your ideal prospect. Every new pixel starts out as a blank slate. First, your pixel must learn about the types of people that are most likely to click to visit your website. Then, it must learn which of your website visitors are most likely to convert. Therefore, even though you are seeking conversions right from the start, it is best to begin with a campaign objective of "Clicks To Website". Once your pixel has recorded 150 conversions, then it will be appropriate for you to switch to a campaign objective of "Website Conversions".

AdSet Setup

AdSets are where you specify your targeting. This is, without a doubt, the single most important aspect of your entire Facebook marketing campaign. Get this right and you will understand exactly how are your prospects are finding your business. Get this wrong and you will very quickly blow your budget and help make the

Zuckerbergs even richer.

First, you must select your geographic targeting. If you're advertising locally, you can choose the size of the radius around your specific location. You also have the option of advertising to specified towns, counties or states. Next, you must select your demographic targeting. Are you marketing to just women over the age of 50 or are you marketing to everybody between the ages of 18 and 30?

Interests comprise the heart of your targeting. Select the ones that are known to resonate with your prospects. For example, a seller of fine, exotic tea might choose to market to people who are interested in very specific, rare types of tea. This seller may also choose to market to individuals who are interested in other luxury tea brands. Facebook Interests are quite specific. Therefore, it is wise to select Interests that are known to your target audience but not necessarily known to the general public.

Facebook Behaviors and Categories offer an additional means of targeting your prospects. With them you can target people that are known, for example, to drive specific types of cars; to make a specific level of income; to use a particular type of device; to be in the market for a specific type of purchase; to have a specific level of education; to be part of a specific subculture; etc. It's a very powerful means of identifying people that may be interested in your offers.

You also have the option of specifying intersections and exclusions in your AdSets. An intersection is defined as a group of people that have more than one interest in common. You can specify that your target audience must like "Interest 1" *and* "Interest 2" in order to be eligible to see your marketing message. Similarly, you can exclude people that have particular interests from seeing your advertisements. You can specify that your target audience must like "Interest 1" but exclude people that like "Interest 3" from that group.

When you are first starting out and testing your various AdSets, start with an initial budget of $10 per per AdSet per day. Believe me, Facebook will find a way to spend the entire amount! With that size of a budget, you will be able to see which AdSets are performing well for you and which ones are not.

When you decide to increase your daily budget, you must NOT raise it more than 20% at a time, and then, do this no more than twice in a single week. Weekly adjustments are better. The reason for this? It gives the Facebook algorithm time to adjust to the new parameters. If you raise your budget too quickly, you will see your previously wonderful stats plummet while your larger budget is spent! Don't be in too much of a hurry to raise your budget. The Facebook algorithm is simply not capable of accurately adjusting to quick budget changes without overspending.

AdSet Size and Placement Types

One of the easiest and most common mistakes is to create an AdSet that is too large. If you have an AdSet with lots and lots of Interests specified, you won't be able to tell which of those Interests are actually bringing in new customers and which ones are just spending your budget fruitlessly. So how large should your AdSets be? I recommend an audience size of no more than 2 million people.

Advanced Facebook marketers will segment a group of interests by placement types.

Meaning, they will create separate AdSets for desktop ads, mobile device ads, Instagram ads and right-column ads. When you do this, you will see that the different placements perform very differently from each other. Some are cheaper. Some may not produce conversions at all.

Ad Creation Formula

1. Reach out
2. State benefits
3. Introduce content, product or service
4. Call To Action
5. Choose images

Start your ad by directly calling out to your prospects and their specific desires. For example, let's say you are marketing telemedicine software to doctors and the decision-makers within a medical practice. Your ad copy should begin with "Are you a doctor or do you manage a medical practice? Would you like to offer your patients the ability to consult face-to-face without leaving the comfort of their home?"

Once you have captured the attention of your prospects, you should state a couple of benefits of your product or service. Just insert one or two sentences here. You are trying to intrigue your prospects just enough so that they will seek additional information by clicking on the ad and visiting your landing page. Finally, introduce your blog post, case study or whitepaper and use a couple sentences to describe the contents. Remember to always write your copy from the perspective of your prospect. Use a call to action to encourage them to view it immediately.

When selecting a supporting image for your ads, it is best to use pictures of people. Even if you are selling a product, use pictures of people enjoying the product itself or enjoying the benefits of using the product. Additionally, make sure that you are using pictures where the people are facing the camera.

If you are marketing an intangible service, it is still advisable to use images of people. These people should be depicted in a happy, relaxed state presumably as a result of using your service. For example, I have successfully used an image of a happy family in a clean home to support an advertisement for a bug exterminator. I have also successfully used an image of a relaxing executive with his feet propped on his desk to support an advertisement for managed network services.

If you are using the Facebook "carousel ad" format, or in other words, the multiple image format, you have the unique opportunity to present multiple features or benefits of your product or service. Of course, each image should support the stated feature or benefit in some way. You will also have the option of sending your prospect to different landing pages based upon the image that they click on. This is useful for promoting multiple products.

Advanced Ad Setup Options

When you are first starting a new campaign, you should be split-testing different ads to determine which one performs the best. Unfortunately, if you create two separate ads and place them within the same Adset, Facebook will not rotate them equally. Therefore, the only way to accurately split-test ads is to duplicate your Adset and place *only one ad within each Adset.* It's sort of tedious, I know, but it's the only way. (Fortunately, Facebook has recently begun rolling out a true split-testing feature for all advertisers to make use of. So you shouldn't have to maintain this tedious process for too much longer.)

If you are using UTM tags to track results

within Analytics (see Chapter 5: How To Track Performance), you will have the option to add them when you are creating your ads. Just scroll down to the bottom of the ad creation interface. You'll see that Facebook gives you the option of adding them there. I recommend using the utm_source tag to denote your Adset and the utm_medium tag to track your ad creative. If you do, your UTM tag will look something like this: utm_source=AdSetName&utm_medium=AdCreati veName

Reporting

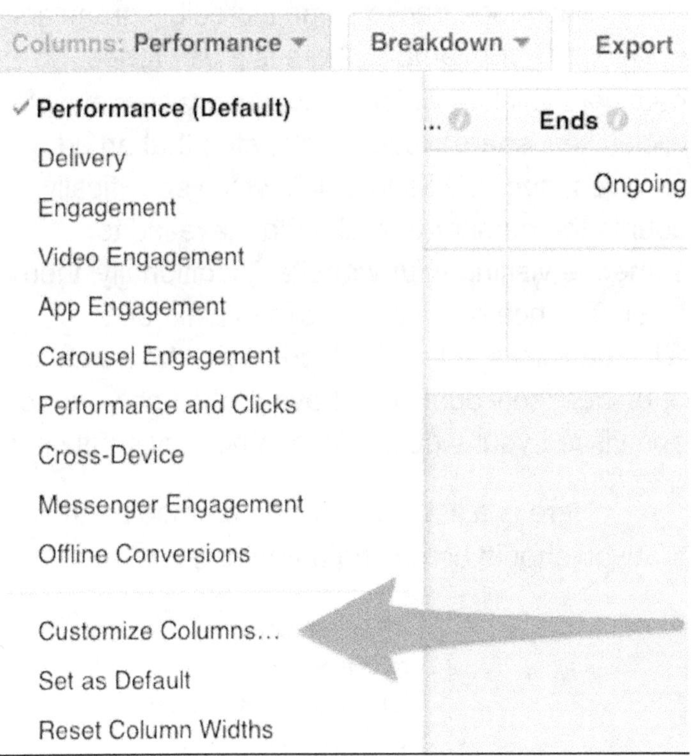

There are many, many important metrics within the Facebook reporting interface that are not immediately visible. You must modify (by selecting "Customize Columns" from the "Performance" menu in your Ad Account interface) your reports in order to gain access to them. It can be daunting, but it is the only way that you will truly know how your AdSets are performing.

Facebook tracks some incredibly granular statistics. For example, there is a difference between “Clicks”, which counts every conceivable click (likes, shares, comments, etc.) that an ad receives, and “Clicks to Link”, which specifically counts the number of clicks that have led to someone visiting your website. Additionally, there is a difference between “Clicks to Link” and “Unique Clicks to Link”, which tracks the number of unique individuals that have clicked on your ad and visited your website. It can be very confusing.

Here is a list of the most common metrics that you should be paying attention to:

- Impressions
- Frequency
- Unique Clicks to Link
- Unique CTR (Link)
- Cost per Unique Click to Link
- Leads
- Cost per Lead
- Purchases
- Cost per Purchase
- Purchase Amount
- Positive Feedback
- Negative Feedback
- Relevance Score

Impressions refers to the number of (pairs of) eyeballs that actually view your ad. Frequency is the *number of times* that a specific prospect views your ad. You need to keep your frequency under 1.5. That way, you won't be wasting ad budget by showing your ad to the same people over and over again. When you notice that your Frequency is above 1.5, you can lower the daily ad spend limit of your AdSet to compensate.

The Unique CTR (Link) is the number of impressions divided by the number of Unique Clicks to Link. The CTR is a terrific indicator of how well your message is resonating with the AdSet. When you start to see Unique CTR (Link) above 1%, you know that you are on the right path.

When someone likes, shares or comments on your ad, those actions will contribute to a high Positive Feedback score. Similarly, when someone chooses to no longer view advertisements from you, that will contribute to a high Negative Feedback score.

Your Relevance Score measures the congruency between the language of your ad and the language of the landing page. So if you have an ad about ice cream but your landing page is about dog food, you will receive a low Relevance Score. This is an important metric to watch, as high Relevance Scores will be rewarded with a lower Cost Per Click.

If you are using video in your advertising, you should watch the metrics related to how many people watch up to 50% over your video, up to 75% of your video, and up to 95% over your video. It will give you a great indicator of where in your video you may need to improve your content.

7 SIMILAR AND LOOKALIKE AUDIENCES

Do you have an email list of prospects or, better yet, do you have an email list of your customers? If you do, then you will greatly benefit by creating Lookalike Audiences in Facebook.

These types of audiences work really well. They are consistently the highest performing and most income generating audiences out of all campaigns. I don't know how the algorithm does it, but I know that Lookalike Audiences are most profitable!

When you create a Lookalike Audience, you are asking Facebook to compile a list of individuals that have the same characteristics and tendencies as the people in your email lists. So if you upload your email list of customers, you will get an audience of people that are highly likely to become your customers. This especially works well when your email lists are segmented based upon the individual products or services purchased. Then you can create a Lookalike Audience full of people that are likely to purchase each product or service.

You can also create an audience based upon the webpages that are visited. So if you're looking for people that are most likely to visit a specific section of your website, just create an audience based upon those that have previously visited that section. Now, what type of audience do you think you'll get when you base it upon those website visitors that land on a 'thank you' or 'purchase successful' page of your website? That's right! You'll get an audience full of people that are likely to convert on your website. Pretty cool, right?

Creating a Lookalike Audience

Creating these audiences are fairly simple. If your customer or prospect list is email based, then you will need that list in a spreadsheet or text file with each email address on a separate line.

Remember to not include the column name in this file.

1. Facebook Lookalike Audiences are created by going to the Audiences section of your Ad Account. First, click on Create Audience and select Custom Audience. Choose the Customer List option and you will be given the opportunity to upload your file and name your new audience.

2. Next, click on Create Audience again and select Lookalike Audience. You will be given the option to choose a Source to base your Lookalike Audience upon. Choose the name of your Custom Audience that you just created. Alternatively, if you wanted to base your Lookalike Audience upon a Custom Audience of website visitors, you can select that audience here as well.

3. Choose a Country from which Facebook will source your new Lookalike audience. If you advertise internationally, then you can create a Lookalike Audience for each country that you are active in.

4. Lastly, you will be given the option to choose a number from 1 to 10 in a section called Audience Size.

Audience size is a very poor description of what is really going on here. If you choose the number 1, yes your audience will be smaller but it will also be comprised of people that are *most similar* to the people on your source list. If you choose the number 10, your audience will be large but won't really resemble or perform like the members of your source list. I will usually create multiple Lookalike Audiences to determine where performance drops off. I recommend starting with Lookalike Audiences of 1% 2% and 3%.

Similar Audiences in Google Analytics

Analytics has a comparable feature known as Similar Audiences. Currently, you aren't allowed to upload email lists but I suspect that this will change in the future. For now, Similar Audiences are created based upon your Google remarketing lists. Since your Google Remarketing lists are based upon your website visitors, it basically means that your Similar Audiences are as well.

There are a couple of additional caveats that you should know about:

1. Similar Audiences can only be based upon Remarketing lists with a

minimum of 500 members.

2. Similar Audiences are only available to be used in the Google Display Network.

These current limitations are only reflecting the fact that Similar Audiences with Google are in the infancy stage. I fully expect this feature to become more robust with the passage of time.

8 PAID TRAFFIC: ADWORDS SEARCH

When someone searches Google for information, Google responds with a search engine results page (SERP). At the very top and very bottom of every SERP is a set of sponsored text ads. These are Search Campaign ads. In this chapter, I am going to guide you through the setup of a Search Campaign.

The Google Adwords Interface

The Google Adwords interface is very complex but very powerful. From within this one interface you can implement:

- Text ads for search engine results pages (SERPs)
- Banner ads for display on other websites or apps

- Video ads for YouTube
- Interactive ads within Gmail
- Remarketing ads
- Product showcase ads from your Ecommerce store

There are so many tabs and submenus in the Adwords interface that I've often referred to it as an endless, four dimensional spreadsheet. Not to worry though, I will help you navigate it.

Structure of a Search Campaign

Your Adwords advertisements have settings available at the Account level, the Campaign level and the Adgroup level. Every Account can contain an infinite number of Campaigns and every Campaign can contain an infinite number of Adgroups.

When you create a setting at the Account level, it will affect every Campaign in your Account. When you create a setting at the Campaign level, it will affect every Adgroup within that Campaign. For example, if you pause a Campaign, then every Adgroup within that Campaign will stop showing ads, even if all of your Adgroups and ads remain unpaused.

It's rare to implement frequent changes to settings at the Account level. But you will often make adjustments at the Campaign and Adgroup level. Campaign settings include the type of campaign you are running, your geographic targeting, your bidding strategy, the time of day that your ads will show and your ad optimization strategy. We'll cover those in the next section.

Adgroups are at the very heart of Adwords. This is where you create your actual ads and also where you select the search queries (known as keywords) that you want to advertise to. For example, if you sell an amazing strawberry ice cream, then you would select the keyword "strawberry ice cream" and create an ad that would display in response to someone searching for that keyword. Adgroups are very important. I will show you how to properly configure your Adgroups soon. But first, we have to create a Campaign to contain your Adgroups.

Search Campaign Setup

When starting a new Campaign, you'll be given options to choose the type of Campaign. One of the biggest mistakes is to choose a hybrid "Search and Display" Campaign. Don't you do it!

There is just too vast of a difference in the setup and performance between them. It ends up being a very costly error for anyone foolish enough to combine them.

1. Create a new Search Only Campaign.

2. Select the option to "Include All Features". This will unlock some of the most powerful capabilities of Adwords and we will make use of them.

3. Choose a name for your Search Only Campaign.

4. Set the geographic targeting for your ads. Local businesses can target by postal code or by a set radius around your location. If your business is more regional, then you can target by city, county or state.

   If you are advertising internationally, I recommend that you organize your Campaigns by country, as each countrys' performance will vary. I've also realized that different countries will speak different dialects of the same language. For example, British people speak a different brand of English than Americans, and both speak it differently than the Australians. It is wise to account for such variances.

5. Locate the menu for Ad Rotation. It's located towards the bottom of the Campaign setup interface.

6. If you are planning on doing any split testing of your ad creative, and I strongly recommend that you do, then you should select the "Rotate Indefinitely" option. This will prevent the Adwords algorithm from interfering with your tests and will give each of your ads an equal number of impressions.

7. Choose how you wish to pay for your ads. Your bidding method choices include:

    a. **CPC (Cost-Per-Click)** This is your best option, especially if you are just starting out. CPC means that you are only paying when someone actually clicks on your advertisement. You must then enter your maximum CPC. It is safe to enter $1 here, as you will have the ability to change this amount later.

b. **CPM (Cost-Per-Mille)** Mille is the Latin word for "one thousand" so a CPM bidding strategy charges you for every 1000 impressions that your ad receives, regardless of whether or not you get clicks.

c. **CPA (Cost Per Action)** Define the amount you are willing to spend for a specified action. CPA bidding works in conjunction with your predefined Analytics Goals and assumes that you already have an idea of how much it costs to acquire an action.

8. Click the "Save and Exit" button at the bottom of the page, as the rest of the options within the Campaign setup interface can be left in their default settings.

Adgroups and Keyword Selection

An Adgroup is a collection of ads and the

keywords that trigger them. You can think of your keywords as the actual search terms that someone enters into the Google search bar. If you Google the phrase "traveling to Japan", then that entire phrase comprises a single keyword. So it's important to remember that a keyword can be made up of more than just a single word.

There are four distinct types of keywords in Google Adwords: Broad Match, Modified Broad Match, Phrase Match and Exact Match. Each type of keyword programs Adwords to respond to search queries in different ways.

1. **Exact Match Keywords** trigger your ad to show only if the search query matches the keyword exactly, *word for word*, without variation. So using the previous example, your ad would show only when the user enters "traveling to Japan". Capitalization is irrelevant.

   Designate your keyword to be Exact Match by enclosing your keyword within brackets.

   Exact Match Example: [traveling to Japan]

2. **Phrase Match Keywords** will trigger the ad to show when the entire keyword appears anywhere within the search query. For example, your ad would appear in response to the query "I want to be traveling to Japan tomorrow" but would not trigger the ad in response to "traveling in Japan".

   Designate your keyword to be Phrase Match by enclosing them in double quotes.

   Phrase Match Example: "traveling to Japan"

3. **Broad Match Keywords** will trigger your ad even if the keyword does not appear in the search query at all! The Adwords algorithm will display your ad if it deems the search query to be closely related to the intent behind your keyword. For example, search terms such as "travel Japan" and "Japanese travel" would possibly trigger your ad. So only use broad match keywords that are quite specific to your products or services.

   Designate your keyword to be Broad

Match Keywords as regular text without any symbols.

Broad Match Example: traveling to Japan

4. **<u>Modified Broad Match Keywords</u>** must appear in the search query. As long as they are in order, Modified Broad Match terms can appear anywhere in a search query and that will trigger your ad. If your Modified Broad Match keyword is +traveling +Japan, then your ads will be triggered by something like "I am traveling and want to be in Japan" but will not be triggered for "in Japan traveling to Osaka".

   It is best to eliminate prepositions and conjunctions from your Modified Broad Match keywords. Meaning, don't worry about words such as in, and, to, or, with, the, for, into, etc. There are just too many possible keyword variations to keep track of that way. So instead of entering +traveling +to +Japan, just enter +traveling +Japan. You'll save precious time in doing so.

Designate your keyword to be Modified Broad Match by adding the plus symbol before each term, without using any spaces.

Modified Broad Match Example: +traveling +Japan

Grouping Keywords into Adgroups

Organizing your Adgroups is the single most important step in setting up your Adwords Search campaign. Get this right and you will have prepared your campaigns for success. Get this wrong and you will lose your ad budget without knowing why.

The worst possible thing that you can do is place all of your keywords into a single Adgroup. There is no better way to destroy your campaign performance than that. Please don't do it! Instead, organize your Adgroups around tightly focused, semantically similar keywords.

For example, let's say that you are an attorney that specializes in family law. First, you should create an Adgroup that contains the keywords "family law attorney" and another Adgroup that contains the keywords "family law lawyer". Next, create Adgroups organized around keywords based upon your products or services. Our family lawyer should create an Adgroup for "divorce lawyer" keywords and another for "child custody attorney" keywords. Within each Adgroup, remember to include each of the four types of keywords.

Each Adgroup has it's own set of ads. By organizing your Adgroups around semantically similar keywords, you will be able to create ads that speak directly to what your prospects are searching for.

Ad Extensions

Although ad Extensions are optional, I definitely recommend that you implement some. Each Extension gives you an extra line of text to work with. The more lines of text your ad has, the greater amount of valuable real estate it will take up on the search engine results page. You want to give yourself the best possible chance to attract the eyeballs of your prospects, right?

Ad Extensions can be added at the Account level, the Campaign level or the Adgroup level. It really depends on how you are going to use them. General messages about your company are best implemented at the Account or Campaign level. Specific messages about individual products or services should be implemented at the Adgroup level.

1. **The Callout Extension**. This Extension adds a line of text directly underneath your headline. It has a size limit of 25 characters. The Callout Extension can be used to display your company's tagline, a sub-headline, or to announce any special offers.

2. **The Review Extension**. If you have any reviews of your business, products or services and they exist online, you can make use of the Review Extension. Let's say you have a review on a third-party website like Yelp or even the New York Times. You can quote your review and the source, and it will appear below your text ad. When creating your Review Extension, you will have to enter the source URL and it will have to be verified, which can take a couple days, before it shows up in your ad.

3. **The Site Link Extension**. Site Links appear below your text ads and can link to a separate section of your website other than the destination URL of your text ad. It's great for promoting specific features of your business or to highlight a variety of products or services. For example, if you're advertising your restaurant and the destination URL takes your visitors to the homepage, you can have site links that take your visitors to a reservation page, a special events page and to the menu page. You can have as little as one Site Link Extension or as many as four.

4. **The Location Extension** is perfect for advertising locally. It displays your business address, phone number and a marker on a local map. On mobile devices, Location Extensions also include a link for the prospect to see directions to your business.

5. **The Call Extension** is available on mobile devices only and enables your prospects to call your business with a single push of a button.

6. **The App Extension.** If you have an app associated with your business, you can implement an App Extension. This Extension will link to your app download page in the Apple store or the Google Play store.

Important Metrics: Tracking Your Conversions

Depending upon how you set up your Goals within Analytics, anything from an email submission to an actual sale can be considered a conversion. Adwords will attribute your conversions to the specific ad and keyword that brought them in. When surveying results from the past month, I recommend that you first look at:

- the number of conversions
- the cost per conversion
- the conversion rate - which is the percentage of website visitors that converted.

If you see a keyword with an abnormally high conversion cost, you should remove it. If you see a keyword that is spending budget without converting, you should remove it. If you are seeing conversion rates that are consistently lower than 10%, you should seek to improve the quality of your landing page.

Important Metrics: CPC, QS and CTR

There are two metrics that greatly determine your overall CPC (Cost-Per-Click). They are the QS (Quality Score) and the CTR (Click-Through-Rate). With a high CTR and a high Quality Score, your CPCs will be exponentially lower. It is Google's way of rewarding relevance and authenticity.

The Quality Score is a number from 1 to 10 that is assigned to each and every keyword. By default, every keyword is initially assigned a value of 6, but that number is adjusted within a couple of days. The Quality Score assesses the relevance of the keyword compared to the language on the landing page.

For example, if you select the keyword "chocolate cake" but your ad is sending traffic to a landing page that is all about hot dogs, your keyword will be assigned a very low Quality Score and your CPC for that keyword will skyrocket. So it is in your best financial interest for your keywords to be congruent with the language of your landing pages.

An ad impression is a single instance of your ad being displayed on a SERP. Your Click-Through-Rate is calculated by dividing the number of clicks that your ad receives by the number of impressions that your ad receives. Really, your CTR is an indicator of how well your advertising message is resonating with your target audience. A CTR of less than 1% demands improvement.

9 PAID TRAFFIC: ADWORDS DISPLAY

Most people think that Display campaigns involve banner ads on third party websites, and for the most part, they are correct. But your banner ads can also appear in mobile apps, and it's not just banners, either. You can place text ads on other websites and in Gmail as well.

There are many different banner ad sizes, but you'll only have to create 3. Those 3 sizes receive over 80% of the impressions available in the Google Display Network. Basically, I'm referring to the most popular horizontal banner ad size, the most popular vertical banner ad size, and the most popular square banner ad size. Their measurements are 728x90, 160x600 and 300x250, respectively.

It is possible to get millions of ad impressions every single day with your Display campaigns. However, since there is so much traffic available in the Google Display Network, it is very important to create separate Adgroups for each traffic source. It's the only way to know if your placements are producing returns on investment or not. So you can definitely expect to have lots of Adgroups in your Display campaigns.

Google Display Campaign Objectives

When you start a new Display Only campaign, you will be taken to a screen where you can give your campaign a name. On that screen, you will be given the option to declare your marketing objectives. Some of the objectives include "Building Awareness", "Influence Consideration", and "Drive Action". If you select one of these objectives, the algorithm will preselect certain advanced options for you. If you are new to Google Display, this may be helpful to you. The algorithm certainly works just fine. However, if you choose not to declare any marketing objective, then you will have all of the advanced options available to you.

Adgroup Targeting Setup

Choosing your Adgroup targeting is most important. Get this right and you will have laser focused, niche specific targeting. Get this wrong and you'll spend your entire ad budget before the sun goes down. This is a complex topic because there are multiple ways that you can target your prospects. You can target them with Keywords, Topics, Placements, Affinities, In-Market Audiences, Remarketing lists, Similar audiences or a combination of these. There are vast amounts of traffic available from each type.

It is vitally important to not place multiple targeting types within the same Adgroup. Choose only one at a time.

Targeting With Topic, Affinity and In-Market Audiences

These are all selected in the same way. You are presented with a drop-down list of categories and should choose the ones that closely match your intended audience.

So, what is the difference between a Topic, an Affinity and an In-Market Audience? Let's say you chose 'Landscape Design' which is a subset of the 'Home and Garden' category.

- Your Topic Adgroup would display your ads on websites that are dedicated to the subject of landscape design.

- Your Affinity Adgroup would display your ads to individuals that are enthusiastic about the subject of landscape design.

- Your In-Market Audience Adgroup would display your ads to individuals that have actively sought to purchase landscape design in the last 7 to 14 days.

Targeting With Keywords

You can also use keywords to target your prospects in a Display campaign. Google will show your ads on pages that rank for a specified keyword. I would advise you to use very specific keywords, as precise as you can get. For example, "auto repair" is too general of a term, but "Audi car repair" is appropriately specific.

The best way to use keywords in a Display campaign is to use them in combination with the other targeting types. If you're selling gourmet green tea, then you naturally would advertise in the "Food & Drink" Affinity category. But even within the "Non-Alcoholic Beverage" subcategory, your ad would be showing up on pages related to coffee, soda and fruit juices. The solution, therefore, is to add the keyword "green tea" to the subcategory. This way, your ads will only appear on pages related to green tea.

Targeting With Placements

Placements allow you to choose the individual websites where you want to show your ads. Do you know of a specific website that would be perfect for your offers? Enter the website URL into the Placement search bar and Google will return a list of available websites that are similar, along with information that will help you make your decision. For example, some websites only display text ads or only banner ads. Other websites aren't mobile friendly. You will see little icons that indicate these facts. Remember to include only one website per Placement Adgroup.

Targeting Gmail Users

Gmail ads have a distinct format that is different and more interactive than regular banner ads or text ads. When you click on "Create Ad", you can find the Gmail ad template to help you setup one. There are 2 parts. The first is the condensed form, featuring a headline, that users initially see. If someone clicks on it, then the ad will increase in size to display the expanded form. This expanded form is like a native ad and can have text and multiple images. You also have the option of customizing the HTML of the expanded version to include multiple links and even forms!

To target Gmail users, create a Placement type of Adgroup and enter mail.Google.com as the URL.

Video Ads

Most people do not realize that YouTube is the second largest search engine in the world behind Google. It's not just for entertainment. It's time for all marketers to realize that YouTube is a vital and valuable source of traffic.

Have you ever been on YouTube, selected a video to watch and seen a small commercial displayed before you can watch your video? This is an option that is available to you from within your AdWords account.

While watching a video on YouTube, have you ever seen some of the “related videos” displayed in the right-hand column? This too is an advertising option available to you.

There is so much traffic in fact, that you will have to be very specific in your targeting to avoid overspending. Although Video Ads are a campaign style of their very own, you will still be using Topics, Keywords, Affinities and In-Market Audiences to target your viewers.

10 REMARKETING

Remarketing is also known as retargeting. The words can be used interchangeably. In order to get the most profit from your online advertising campaigns, you *need* to be remarketing.

Have you ever had an ad follow you around the Internet? For example, let's say you found a nice pair of boots online, but you didn't buy them. All of a sudden, your boots are showing up in advertisements on just about every webpage that you visit. That's remarketing!

The science of marketing states that your prospects need multiple touch points with your company before they decide to buy. Remarketing allows you to provide those additional touch points. These are customized messages that are based upon the previous actions of your website visitors. To your prospects, the message will feel personalized, which will increase the chances that they will make a purchase.

> How does remarketing work? When someone visits your website, the remarketing script places a little piece of code, known as a cookie, into the browser of your website visitor. When your prospect visits a different website, another script reads the cookie and automatically serves an appropriate ad.

Best Practices for Remarketing List Creation

The two most common remarketing platforms are Facebook and Google. You should be able to remarket to all of your website visitors through them. Of course, the implementation process for each platform is very different, but you will be creating the same audiences in each.

First, create remarketing lists of all visitors to your website, organized by 30 day intervals: A general list of visitors from the past 30 days; a general list of visitors from the past 60 days; a general list of visitors from the past 90 days; etc.

For most e-commerce websites, your prospects are most likely to make a purchase within 15 days of coming to your site. So you should create a series of remarketing messages to capitalize on this trend. Create a remarketing list for people that have visited your site in the last 5 days. Next, create a list for those that visited up to 10 days ago. Finally, create a list for prospects that were on your website no more than 15 days ago. If you have a longer sales cycle, then you may have to alter the lists to reflect that longer cycle, perhaps creating 10 day intervals instead.

You might be thinking, "aren't people that visited my website in the past 10 also part of the group of visitors from the past 15 days? How do I make sure that each group sees the right message?"

The answer is simple: When you create an AdSet in Facebook or an AdGroup in AdWords, you will target one remarketing list and exclude another remarketing list from it. For example, you will be able to include the remarketing list of visitors from the past 15 days and exclude the remarketing list of visitors from the past 10 days.

This will create a subset of people that have been on your website in the past 11 to 15 days.

Of course, the beauty of remarketing lies not only in targeting people that have visited your website within a certain time frame, but in targeting visitors to sections or even specific pages of your website. I'm going to show you how to set up those remarketing lists now. One quick note: It is not necessary to organize these lists by time intervals. Just create the list to include every visitor for the maximum (180 days) allowable time frame. If you want to remarket to section-specific visitors based upon time intervals, we can easily create an intersection between section-specific remarketing lists and time-interval specific remarketing lists.

Hopefully, your website is divided into categories of your offerings. For example, if you sell clothes, your hats should all be contained in the YourDomain.com/hats directory. If so, you can easily use the "Contains" option (see Chapter 5 for an explanation) to create an audience of visitors that have viewed your selection of hats.

Next, create remarketing lists for anyone that has successfully purchased or opted in to one of your offers. You can do this by identifying the specific URL for the "purchase successful" page or "thank you" page.

Most importantly, create a remarketing list for anyone that has abandoned their shopping cart. This is done by including anyone that has visited any page in the checkout process (or anyone that has pressed the "Add to Cart" button) and excluding anyone that has visited the "purchase successful" page.

Remarketing List Setup in Facebook

Creating remarketing lists in Facebook is a fairly straightforward process. Start by going to the "Audiences" section of your Facebook Ad Account. Click on the blue "Create Audience" button and select the "Custom Audience" option. You'll be creating an audience based upon "Website Traffic".

You'll see a menu with audience creation options that are self explanatory:

Website Traffic | Anyone who visits your website ▾

In the Last | 30 days

✓ Include past website traffic

Audience Name | Enter a name for your audience

Add a description

Depending upon which option you choose, you may be given the opportunity to define the specifics of the webpage URLs that you wish to base your audience upon. For example, if you were creating the audience for those cart-abandoning prospects that have begun but not completed the checkout process, you may define it by including URLs that contain “checkout” but exclude URLs that contain “order-confirmation”. Of course, this does depend upon the specifics of your shopping-cart software and individual checkout process. Your web developer can assist with this.

Website Traffic | People visiting specific web pages but not others

Include people who visit any web page that meets the following rules.

URL contains | Add URL keywords

Exclude people who visit any web page that meets the following rules.

URL contains | Add URL keywords

In the Last | 30 days

✓ Include past website traffic

Audience Name | Enter a name for your audience

Add a description

Remarketing List Setup in Analytics

Remarketing with Google is accomplished by utilizing a combination of Analytics and Adwords. Have you linked your Analytics and Adwords accounts? If not, refer to Chapter 5 for instructions on how to do it.

You will setup your remarketing lists in Analytics. But be forewarned! Analytics is much more precise, powerful and complicated than setting up Facebook Audiences because you can populate a list based upon any metric that is tracked by Analytics. That means that you could segment users by age, gender, operating system, browser type/version, traffic source, ad campaign, website page, and hundreds of other variables.

Login to your Analytics account and click on the Admin tab. You should see the "Audience Definitions" option. Click it and select "Audiences". The first time you do this, you must confirm the "Destination Account" as your own Adwords account.

From there, you will be given the option to Define your Audience. Select the option "Users who visited a specific section of my site" and it will pull up a submenu for you to input your specific webpages.

That wasn't too bad, was it? Now, the next time you are in your Adwords account, you will be able to remarket by creating AdGroups that are based upon the lists that you have just created.

Remarketing Messages

Remarketing messages can be created to serve many different objectives. They can offer additional information about your brand or specific products. They can offer a special discount. They are especially useful for the situation where a prospect places an item into their shopping cart but then abandons it before purchasing. Some businesses remarket exclusive offers to existing customers. Others remarket to reengage prospects that haven't visited the website in over a month.

Advanced remarketers create *a series of messages* based upon how long it has been since the prospect visited the website. Every few days, the message changes! If you've created your remarketing lists according to my instructions in this chapter, you will be able to do just that.

Do you remember Aristotle from your history class? The Greek philosopher wrote a book on the subject of persuasion called "On Rhetoric". In it, he describes a 3-fold approach to creating persuasive arguments: Ethos, Pathos and Logos. This approach works very well in the context of remarketing. Allow me to explain.

Ethos translates as "character" and is used as a means of establishing your credibility and trustworthiness. If an authority such as a doctor recommends your product, using that endorsement is a good example of including ethos into your marketing message.

Pathos translates as "suffering" or "sensation" and is used in persuasion as an appeal to the emotions of your prospect. You can use this positively, by invoking the state of your customers after using your product or service, or negatively by focusing on the frustrations that your prospect feels by not having the solution that your product or service offers. In other words, you can appeal to your prospects' hopes & dreams or fears & worries.

Logos, in direct contrast to pathos, translates as "reason". When you use numbers and facts to support your arguments, you are invoking logos.

Using credibility, logic and emotional content as a basis for each of your individual remarketing messages will greatly enhance their persuasiveness and effectiveness. It's a brilliant strategy that has been in use for over 2,400 years. I'll bet you didn't know you were going to get a history lesson today, did you?

11 EMAIL MARKETING STRATEGIES

Despite all of the advancements in Internet marketing, email marketing remains the backbone of profitability in online business. When someone gives you their email address, it is an invitation into their private space and it allows you to engage in a more personal outreach with your prospects and customers.

Did you know that it is common practice for most online marketers to make little or no profit from the initial sale? In most cases, the initial sale simply recoups the cost of advertising. But once these marketers are in possession of an email address, they can begin to follow up with backend offers for products and services that are quite profitable.

When you have developed a warm relationship with the members of your email list, not only can you make money from selling your own products and services, but you can also generate income from offering affiliate offers as well. However, some Internet marketers do not develop warm relationships with their email lists and can still make money. They do it by renting access to their list on a per email basis. All of this underscores the importance of having and curating your own list of email addresses.

Segmentation

It is best to segment your email lists into sub-lists that are defined by past behaviors. People that have purchased products should be segmented from those that have not. People that have recently opened your emails should be segmented from those that appear inactive. If you're an affiliate marketer (someone that promotes anothers' products in exchange for earning a commission), your lists should be segmented according to the types of offers that people appear interested in.

With the right customer relations management (CRM) software or the right email service provider, your lists can be segmented automatically. If you are an established online marketer, all-in-one platforms such as Infusionsoft or Ontraport can handle these tasks for you. But those are expensive options and come with a steep learning curve. If you run a small business or are just starting out, then I wholeheartedly recommend using Active Campaign to send emails, to automate sending sequences, to test headlines and to segment your lists.

Deliverability – Avoiding The Spam Folder

Deliverability is an important email marketing topic. If you are sending multiple emails over a short period of time, your messages can easily end up in the spam folder. The easiest and best way to avoid this is to ask your recipients to add your sending email address to either their address book or their 'safe senders' list. That way, they can ensure that they will receive all of your messages. It doesn't hurt to ask, right?

Indeed. Large ISPs (Internet Service Providers) notice which senders are being added to safe lists and which senders are being added to spam folders. So even if one recipient takes no action, the fact that others are adding your sending email address to their safe list does influence whether your messages end up in the inbox or the spam folder.

Split-Testing

Smart email marketers are constantly split-testing their emails to improve performance. You can begin by testing different subject lines to see which one improves your open rates. When your open rate rises above 30%, then you know you have a winning message in your subject line. You should also split-test the content of your emails and measure performance by the rate that your recipients click through to seek additional information on your website. A click through rate (CTR) of 6% is considered healthy.

Unsubscribes

Naturally, some of your recipients may seek to unsubscribe from your list. Don't worry, this is perfectly normal. As you have the ability to customize your unsubscribe page, you should view this moment as an opportunity. You could offer additional downloadable resources for free. You could offer the choice to unsubscribe from one sub-list while remaining on others. You could seek input for the reason they unsubscribe so that you can better tailor your messages in the future. It is really up to you but, at the very least, you should wish your subscriber well. They may one day return to seek your advice, services or products in the future.

Automation Sequences

I'm going to outline 2 basic email sequences that have proven effective in marketing products and services. The first is a 3-step sequence that presents your product or service from 3 distinct vantage points. The second is a 7-step sequence that utilizes social proof, empathy and engagement to persuade your prospects into buying.

As always, you should present your product or service from the viewpoint of your prospective customer. It means you're not talking about your offers. Instead, you are talking about how your offer solves the problem that your prospect is currently experiencing.

The 3-Step Email Sequence

1. In your first email, you should articulate, in as much detail as possible, the benefits that your prospect will gain as a result of purchasing

your offer. How will your new customer experience life differently? How will your new customer feel? In this email, you should use descriptive language and words that arouse the emotional satisfaction that your prospects crave.

2. In contrast, your second email should be fact-based and rational. You should still describe how your new customer experiences life differently as a result of purchasing your offer, but you are doing so from a logical point of view. Whenever possible, you should use statistics and exact numbers to support and underscore your arguments.

3. Finally, your third email should exacerbate the current problem situation that your offer alleviates. You should elaborate on the frustrations that your prospects will continue to find themselves experiencing. Describe the consequences of not acting upon your (time sensitive?) offer and implore your prospects to choose a different path.

I must warn you. This email sequence is incredibly powerful. It will generate massive sales from those prospects that understand the wisdom behind your arguments. But it will generate a backlash from the stubborn fools that do not. This is to be expected and is an indicator that your marketing messages are on point. The intention of successful marketing is to elicit a response and a decision from your prospects. Sometimes that response is positive and sometimes it is not.

The 7-Step Email Sequence

The 7-step email sequence employs the concept of open and closed loops. Have you ever experienced a cliffhanger at the end of a television show, book chapter or movie? Some curious situation arises that demands resolution. You must know what happens next. That is an example of opening the loop. As the story progresses, the situation reaches a conclusion (the loop is closed) and all questions are answered.

For this sequence, I am assuming that you have collected the email address of a prospect in exchange for a downloadable PDF or access to an informative video or something like that.

1. In the first email of your 7-step sequence you should begin by welcoming your prospect and perhaps acknowledging their search for a solution to their problem. Next, you should ask if they have

successfully accessed your free resource. Provide them with a link to it, just in case. Finally, you should open a loop and mention that they can expect to receive an email "tomorrow" that reveals a case study of someone that has achieved a breakthrough as a result of purchasing and using your product or service.

2. Your second email, as promised, should close the loop and deliver a case study. At the end of this email, you should place a link to your sales page. Start your case study by describing the attitudes and needs of your prospects before they purchased your product or service. Then chronicle the specific details of the transformation process. Finally, illustrate the tangible results that your customer enjoys as a result of putting your products or services to good use.

3. Your third and fourth emails could be characterized as traditional "Problem-Agitate-Solve" style emails. Start your third email by detailing the problem your prospects currently experience and agitate the situation by expounding on how they typically deal with it. Then, present your offer as a means of eradicating the problem. Finish your third email by opening a loop that promises to outline the consequences of

not taking action.

4. Start your fourth email by closing the loop and focusing on the misery of having the same problem for an extended period of time. Agitate the situation with a description of the money and opportunities lost. Present your offer as a means of reclaiming all of that wasted time, money and opportunity.

5. Your fifth email will take an entirely different tone. You see, not only do your prospects want a solution to their problem, they also desire the satisfaction and empowerment that comes with having solved the problem. This is what your fifth email should characterize. Your writings should extensively elaborate on the subtle longings of your prospect to solve the problem once and for all. Don't forget to include a link to your sales page at the end!

6. Your sixth email should also deliver a case study, although there should be some obvious differences between this one and the case study that you sent in your second email.

I'm sure you realize that not all of your prospects are exactly the same. Some might be beginners in your industry while others may be more experienced. Each group of prospects will have different perspectives and a distinct profile. Your second case study should reflect and address the concerns of this second subset of your prospects.

7. Your seventh and final email in the series should include a summary of the previous 6 emails plus an invitation to engage. You could ask your prospects why they haven't purchased yet and instruct them to reply. You could offer a free 15 minute consultation if that is possible. You could invite them to take a survey, receive additional information or enter a contest. It is entirely up to you. The point is to seek one final action from your prospect to somehow keep them engaged with your business.

Sources of Email Lists

If you have an offer or an email sequence that is proven to convert prospects into customers, you may wish to send it to as many email addresses as possible. There are a number of ways to gain access to other peoples email lists. That's what this section is about.

When evaluating which lists you should or shouldn't purchase access to, it is important to keep certain details in mind. Most list owners will have detailed demographic information available about their lists, but the following metrics are critical. Every reputable list owner should know the Open Rate of the list. Every reputable list owner should know the Click Through Rate (CTR) of the list. Most importantly, every reputable list owner should know the EPC, or Earnings Per Click of the list. Armed with this knowledge, you should be able to calculate if investing in the list is worth the asking price.

Professional associations are great sources of email lists. So are chambers of commerce and business journals. All types of magazines and periodicals sell access to their email lists. Think about the various niche-specific publications, both online and off-line, where your prospects may seek information and entertainment.

You can also work directly with an email list brokerage service. List brokers usually have access to email lists that just aren't publicly available. Two of the most reputable list brokerages are Dedicated Emails and Flat Iron Media.

Chapter Summary

- Develop warm relationships with your list.
- Segment your lists according to past user behaviors.
- Make sure your messages make it into the inbox.
- Split-test your subject lines and content.
- Measure your Open Rates and Click Through Rates.
- Have a plan for Unsubscribes.
- Use the 3-Step and 7-Step Email Sequences.
- Seek additional sources of email lists.
- Use metrics like Open Rates, CTRs and EPC to discern bad investments from good investments.

12 AUTOMATION

I want to briefly introduce you to the concept of automation. It is important because anytime that you can get computers and software to perform repetitive tasks, you are streamlining your business into greater efficiency. Automation is how you get more work done with less effort.

Of course, there are dozens if not hundreds of platforms that automate specific processes. For example, you can use landing page builders to automate the process of split testing. And most email service providers offer some degree of automation when it comes to sending emails and segmenting your lists.

However, the real champions of Internet marketing automation are Zapier and IFTTT. Both of these services integrate with hundreds of online platforms to perform customized, cross-platform, automated routines on demand.

Let's say your payment processor has a clunky reports generator. You can program Zapier or IFTTT to automatically add all purchase data from your payment processor to a Google spreadsheet in real time. After that, you can have it programmed so that you automatically receive a text message indicating that you have just made a sale.

Zapier and IFTTT work with email service providers, accounting softwares, Google services, CRMs and a wide variety of online service providers. They can help you with your onboarding process, customer service, email list segmentation, or with any repetitive task that you require. The possibilities are staggeringly endless.

So go ahead and say goodbye to time wasting, menial, repetitive tasks. Say hello to modern day business productivity.

www.ingramcontent.com/pod-product-compliance
Lightning Source LLC
Chambersburg PA
CBHW071443180526
45170CB00001B/439

* 9 7 8 1 5 4 2 3 7 1 3 7 7 *